D0778568

DEEP BLUES

DEEP BLUES

BILL TRAYLOR, SELF-TAUGHT ARTIST

MARY E. LYONS

CHARLES SCRIBNER'S SONS · NEW YORK
Maxwell Macmillan Canada · Toronto
Maxwell Macmillan International
New York · Oxford · Singapore · Sydney

ACKNOWLEDGMENTS

I am grateful to the following for their help: Charles and
Eugenia Shannon; Frank Maresca of the Frank Maresca/Roger
Ricco Gallery; Hirschl & Adler Modern; Scott DeVeaux; and
especially Judy Saslow, whose generosity made it possible to
bring the story of Bill Traylor to young readers.

Charles Scribner's Sons Books for Young Readers
Macmillan Publishing Company
866 Third Avenue, New York, NY 10022

Maxwell Macmillan Canada, Inc.
1200 Eglinton Avenue East, Suite 200
Don Mills, Ontario M3C 3N1

Macmillan Publishing Company is part of the
Maxwell Communication Group of Companies.

First edition   10 9 8 7 6 5 4 3 2 1
Printed in Hong Kong on recycled paper
Book design by Vikki Sheatsley

Library of Congress Cataloging-in-Publication Data
Lyons, Mary (Mary E.)
   Deep blues : Bill Traylor, self-taught artist /
Mary E. Lyons. — 1st ed.   p.   cm.
   Includes bibliographical references and index.
   ISBN 0-684-19458-9
1. Traylor, Bill, 1854–1947—Juvenile literature.   2. Afro-
American painters—Alabama—Biography—Juvenile litera-
ture.   3. Primitivism in art—Alabama—Juvenile literature.
[1. Traylor, Bill, 1854–1947. 2. Artists. 3. Afro-Americans—
Biography.]   I. Traylor, Bill, 1854–1947. II. Title.
ND237.T617L96 1994   759.13—dc20   [B]   93-23736

SUMMARY: The life and accomplishments of a twentieth-
century African-American folk artist (African-American Artists and Artisans series).

To the memory of Bill Traylor

Photograph by Charles Shannon.

Bill Traylor was born into slavery near the village of Benton, Alabama. Benton sits like a buckle in the center of the Black Belt. This wide strip of dark, sticky clay stretches across the waistline of three Deep South states: Louisiana, Mississippi, and Alabama.

Before the Civil War, hundreds of cotton plantations dotted the rolling ridges of Alabama's Black Belt. George Traylor, a slaveholder, owned one of these large farms. It was here that Bill was born in 1856.

Bill came into the world with little to call his own. Even his last name was a hand-me-down, a cast-off coat that he wore for the rest of his life. Many years later, he still had few belongings. As one former Alabama slave said of his own poverty, "I ain't got nothin', I ain't got nothin', I ain't got nothin'."

But by the end of his life, Bill was rich in other ways. He had fathered a large family and had many grandchildren. After years of illiteracy, he had learned to write his name. And he had created over 1,200 pieces of delightful art for the world to enjoy.

For most of his ninety-three years, he was a farmer. From his pictures, however, we can see what else he might have been: architect, dancer, musician, or portrait painter. Looking at Bill Traylor's art is like walking into a hall of mirrors. Everything seems simple at first, but the possibilities are endless.

SLAVERY

"I wonder, Lord, will I ever get to heaven
to walk them golden streets."

Alabama "shout"

Bill never planned to be an artist. When he was growing up, however, his artist's eye recorded the houses, animals, trees, and people that he saw in the Alabama countryside. He saved these memories for a later season, like a pile of cotton seeds set aside for spring planting. Finally, in the autumn of Bill's life, the memories blossomed into pictures.

One of Bill's strongest recollections was of his family's cabin. Most Alabama slave cabins were sixteen feet by eighteen feet. Families of five or six slept in the one-room log or plank dwellings. There wasn't much furniture—as shown in Bill's paintings, usually just a simple table and a chair or two.

Young Bill's chores might have included scrubbing the inside of his cabin and whitewashing the outside. But even these tiresome jobs could not improve the rough shanties. "They wasn't fitten for nobody to live in," said an Alabama ex-slave. "We just had to put up with them."

For many decades after the Civil War, African-American tenant farmers and sharecropping families lived in similar houses. When Bill began to draw, these same buildings appeared in many of his paintings.

Like most cabins in Bill's time, *Yellow and Blue House* rests on blocks a foot above the ground. Its two rooms are separated by a dogtrot, or covered breezeway. During slavery times, the chimneys would have been made of clay and sticks. The metal pipe that peeks out of the roof vents smoke from a woodstove.

Bill's picture tells us that he lived in a simple house. It also shows a droll humor that helped him through difficult times. Big hats, hooked noses, and bulging chins give the men a comic look. The figure on the roof dances daintily with a bird. Another rocks below, one jaunty leg hiked into the air. Magically, the arm of the seated man has become the arm of his chair.

When Bill was a child he spent more time outdoors than inside the cabin. His mother probably carried him to the fields each morning, since 80 percent of Alabama's female

slaves were field hands. She would have put Bill in a sling, then tied the sling to a tree limb to keep ants and bugs from chewing on his tender skin. One former slave remembered that his mother left him in the shade of an oak tree while she plowed. "There I sat all day," he said, "and that tree was my nurse."

Branches sprout in many of Bill's drawings. They show that he felt a strong kinship with trees. As a boy, he would have played in the pure stands of cedar that grew in the Black Belt. When he shook persimmon trees in the fall, mushy balls of tart fruit fell at his feet. And the smooth bark of a pine tree was as familiar to Bill as his own skin; in rural Alabama, there were more longleaf pines than people.

In *Dancing Cauldron* a pair of legs turns mysteriously into a treetop. In Bill Traylor's natural world, people can look like plants, and animals can act like humans. As the cat dangles in midair, we see desperation in its wide eye. But the cartoonlike animal makes

A typical Black Belt cabin was made of foot-wide upright boards and surrounded by a picket fence. Packed dirt around the house was swept every day with a broom of dogwood branches tied with string. As in West Africa, a neat yard had no grass. *Yellow and Blue House, ca. 1939–1942. Pencil and colored pencil on cardboard. 22" x 14". Collection of Judy Saslow.*

The erasures show that Bill experimented until the lines of the drawing pleased him. *Dancing Cauldron, ca. 1939–1942. Charcoal on cardboard. 9" x 8¼". Private collection. Courtesy Luise Ross Gallery, New York.*

us smile. Cats are seldom afraid of heights, so we know its fear isn't real.

The same picture reveals the importance of shoes to the artist. Shoes would have been rare in Bill's childhood years. If he wore any at all, they were rough brogans. Alabama slaves called these "red russets," perhaps because the leather was the color of a red potato. The stiff leather never softened. When the shoes rubbed blisters, Bill might have split them down each side to keep his feet from hurting. On Sundays he would have cleaned the brogans with hog gristle before going to "bresh" church meetings in the woods. Or he may have hung them over the top of the chimney until they were "polished" black with soot.

Like most Black Belt planters, George Traylor raised cotton on his 388 acres. He also built his own cotton gin, or engine. When Bill was a small boy, he watched the mule-powered gin pull black seeds from their soft homes inside each cotton boll. After the fluffy white cotton was ginned, it was pressed into bales for shipment to market.

Bill's mother may have let him walk over to the nearby banks of the Alabama River, where he would have stood at the top of a long wooden slide called a chute. From this point, high above the river, he could watch older boys push bales of cotton down the chute to a steamboat waiting below.

Since Bill was only five when the Civil War began, he probably didn't work in the fields until the war was over. Still, even young children had to help with farm labor in some way. As a water boy for field hands, he would have fetched buckets of water from a nearby spring. And he surely gathered lightwood, or kindling, for the cabin fireplace several times a day.

Before the Civil War, George Traylor handed out food every Saturday to Bill's family. Most slave rations included only the bare necessities. Each adult was allowed a few pounds of hog meat, a peck (eight quarts) of

Cotton chute located on the Alabama River near the town of Claiborne. The roof covers two sections: steps on the left and a chute made of smooth planks on the right. *Ballou's Pictorial Drawing-Room Companion, April 21, 1855. Courtesy Special Collections, Alderman Library, University of Virginia.*

As a boy, Bill would have heard that a hog "piling trash," or running with branches in its mouth, was a sign of bad weather. *Black Pig, ca. 1939–1942. Poster paint and pencil on cardboard. 11" x 14". Collection of Judy Saslow.*

cornmeal, sweet potatoes, syrup made from sorghum grain, and buttermilk.

Bill's mother probably had a small garden of cabbage, collards, and onions. Her vegetables and wild game from his father's Saturday-night hunting trips helped break the monotony of pork and corn bread.

The whole family looked forward to a Sunday treat of biscuits and coffee with sugar. Christmas meant chicken and perhaps deer meat to eat. But pork was the basic, day-in,

day-out fare. Pigs were part of Bill's chores as well as his diet. He built their pens, fed them, chased them, and helped with hog killings in the fall.

Years later Bill plopped these same hogs down on paper. *Black Pig* is almost as big as a set-down hog. According to a former Alabama slave, a set-down hog was a pig that "done ate so much corn [and] he got so fat that he feets can't hold him up and he just set on he hind quarters and grunts and eats

and eats and grunts." Chasing a set-down hog wasn't necessary, the ex-slave remembered. He simply knocked the poor fat creature on its head.

At best the food that the slaves ate was plentiful, although it lacked the vitamins and minerals they needed to stay healthy. At worst there simply wasn't enough to eat. By the end of the Civil War, Bill and his family would have been hungrier than ever before. They must have looked back on prewar rations as if they had been princely feasts.

THE CIVIL WAR

"Fire on the quarter-deck, fire on the bow
Fire on the gun-deck, fire down below."

Steamboat work song

In April 1861, five-year-old Bill saw the northern lights skip over the night skies of Alabama. The strange lights were caused by solar flares, but some thought they were a sign of victory for the Confederate States. Others said they were an evil omen of defeat.

To add to their food supply, Black Belt farmers often hunted possums and wild turkeys. *Possum Hunt, ca. 1939–1942. Poster paint and pencil on cardboard. 24" x 13⅛". Collection of Judy Saslow.*

The Confederacy was a group of seven Southern states that had withdrawn from the United States of America, then declared war on it. The Southerners were fighting so that they could own people as property.

Bill was still a "shirttail" child: so little that he ran naked or wore only a long shirt with no pants. He was too young to care one way or the other about the Civil War. But the outcome changed his small world forever. When the fighting was over, the town of Benton and the Traylor plantation would never be the same.

Before the outbreak of war, steamboats glided up and down the Alabama River. During high-water season, the captain made regular stops at small landings like Benton to pick up cotton and more passengers. The tubalike sound of a steam whistle cried Wake up! to Bill each morning. The same rude blast announced his bedtime at night. But by 1865 the river was quiet, the boats destroyed by Union shells.

Benton was a small village of about ten merchants when the war started. Bill probably went to town once a week with a grown-up, where he stood on tiptoe to peep through the windows of the Mansion House Hotel.

His nose turned toward the sweet smells that drifted from the bakery. And he was fascinated by the machine shop, mill works, and livery stable. The dentist's office and drugstore, however, held no interest for a little boy like Bill. By the end of the war, most of these businesses were gone.

On April 9, 1865, ten thousand Union cavalrymen left Selma, Alabama, on horseback. Led by General James Wilson, the dark blue cloud of soldiers thundered toward Montgomery. Twelve miles outside of Selma, some of Wilson's men passed through Benton. They burned much of the little village. Then a few of the men strayed onto the Traylor plantation.

The Union soldiers were fighting against slavery. But many slaves were terrified of the invading Northern army. Bill and his family must have watched with fear as Wilson's raiders stalked through George Traylor's house. The soldiers sacked the smokehouse and ruined the meat by rolling it in black dirt. Then they burned the cotton gin and one hundred bales of cotton. It's likely that they also destroyed farm animals such as chickens, cows, horses, and mules.

The Confederacy lost the war, and Bill and

Cotton bales moved slowly down the chute at first, then picked up speed and landed on the deck with enough force to shake the entire boat. *Ballou's Pictorial Drawing-Room Companion, April 21, 1855. Courtesy Special Collections, Alderman Library, University of Virginia.*

his family were finally free from enslavement. But they soon faced another kind of bondage: starvation. During the last year of the war, a bushel of corn had cost thirteen dollars in Alabama. Rations for slaves had been reduced to cornmeal, bacon, syrup, and "coffee" brewed from weeds.

After the war the United States government started the Freedmen's Bureau. Branches were located all over the South. The bureau helped former slaves by providing food, clothing, and schools. Rations were issued three times a week, but supplies reached only some of the African-American population.

In isolated places like Benton, people lived on blackberries, green corn, and pure gumption.

RECONSTRUCTION

"Eeoho-eeoho-eeoho-weioho-i!"

Cotton-field holler

When the war was over, nine-year-old Bill remained on the Traylor farm. His family may have felt that was the best place to fight the new battle against hunger. But many other freed people threw down their hoes. They moved to Alabama towns or to cities farther north: Cincinnati, Cleveland, Detroit. Some had to leave because the farms were abandoned. In Bill's county alone, white landowners couldn't pay taxes on fifty thousand acres.

The joyful leaving had a dark side. Some freed people who moved away became homeless wanderers. They lived in ruined houses or sheds. Others slept under bridges or in caves along the riverbanks. Bill's mother and father must have thought it was better to stay on the land than to starve in the city.

We don't know exactly how Bill's family survived the years after the Civil War. Since they decided to remain, conditions on George Traylor's plantation might have been better than most. Or perhaps they were too frightened to leave. In the 1860s Alabama was infested with more Ku Klux Klan members than any other Southern state. The KKK terrorized former slaves with kidnappings and lynchings. They wanted to frighten blacks into staying to farm the land.

Many freed people did become farm laborers. They lived in the landowners' cabins and worked their fields for daily cash wages. When the growing season was over, they moved to cities for winter jobs. Some found work on the railroad or in lumber camps.

But the typical African-American Black Belt farmer was a sharecropper. He worked a "one-horse farm on halves." This meant he planted about fifteen acres of cotton for half the profit. Each spring, the landowner lent him tools, a mule, seeds, and fertilizer. In the fall the landowner subtracted the cost of these supplies from the farmer's share of the profit.

Sharecropping was a tricky business. Most ex-slaves couldn't read, write, add, or subtract. Only the landlord knew the price of cotton and how much the family owed him for supplies. It was easy to cheat sharecroppers, and many finished the year with little or no cash.

Some sank into hopeless debt to the land-owners. As one Black Belt farmer complained, "Seem like I ain't never break even." When this happened they moved to another plantation and another plot of land. "The only way to get out of debt," Alabama sharecroppers used to say, "is to walk out."

The best way to save money was to become a tenant. Tenants paid rent for their cabins and land with cash or part of the cotton crop. They had to supply their own mules and farming tools. But after they had paid the rent, all profit belonged to the tenants and their families.

Bill grew up on the Traylor plantation and remained there for most of his life. He lived in a cabin by a creek. And like his parents before him, he was probably a tenant, share-cropper, or laborer.

When Bill was twenty-nine, George Traylor died. George's nineteen-year-old son, Marion, became owner of the farm. Marion's field notes show that Bill worked as a flag, or pole, man for him when the land was surveyed in 1888. Bill certainly needed the extra income. In that year, at the age of thirty-two, he had a wife, Lorisa, and four children to feed.

The hand on hip, relaxed knee, and slouch hat give this Alabama Black Belt farmer a jaunty look. The same pose can be seen in many of Bill Traylor's pictures, along with the ladder, mule, and picket fence. *University of Chicago Press.*

In this visual joke the logo of the Foldomatic shirt cardboard becomes a navel. *Mother and Child, ca. 1939–1942. Pencil and colored pencil on cardboard. 15½" x 11¾". Collection of Judy Saslow.*

FAMILY

"Ten policemen all dressed in blue,
    comin' down the street two by two,
    lookin' for Railroad Bill."

Alabama ballad

Bill once said that he had raised twenty children. Mothers often died in childbirth in rural Alabama, so he may have married twice and had two sets of children. He might also have taken in some of his brothers' and sisters' offspring. Black Belt kinfolk frequently loved, adopted, and raised one another's children.

From the 1900 census we know that Bill and Lorisa's oldest living child, Pauline, was born in 1884. After Pauline they had at least six more girls and three more boys.

In those days big families were not unusual. More children meant more help on the farm, especially at harvest time.

The death rate for children was high, however. Stillbirths and disease often turned a large family into a small one. One Black Belt parent recalled, "I was the mother of fifteen children in all. I got six living. Some come live, but didn't live no time, yet three got to be big children walking about before they dies."

For Bill and Lorisa, life stretched out like countless rows of cotton. In the quiet countryside around Benton, one year was much like the next. In March Bill would have plowed the ground and planted cotton and corn. From April through August he and the older children got up at 5:00 A.M. to eat a breakfast fixed by Lorisa. Then they all hoed and weeded until the sun heated the air to a quivering 115 degrees. "The sun was so hot," remembered a Black Belt farmer's daughter, "you could see little devils twinkling out in front of you." In the fall the family would have dug sweet potatoes, picked peanuts, and chopped cotton.

Bill was a responsible farmer. In the winter he moved wagonloads of leaf mold from the woods to the fields. This enriched the soil and resulted in better crops. A mule pulled the plow as Bill mixed the rich organic matter into the dirt.

A cotton crop brought more cash, but Bill tried to raise as much food as he could. "You could have that building over there full of money," he once said, "but you couldn't eat it." For most Black Belt farmers like Bill and Lorisa, farming was a life-or-death affair. If they didn't grow food, they didn't eat.

And without a mule, they didn't grow food. Bill's many pictures of mules show that these stubborn animals were as real as people to him. He fed his mule, fought with him, depended on him. "He hear something," Bill once described a mule he had drawn. "Come up on one at night and he'll sure see you before you see him."

Of another painting of a mule Bill said, "He's sullen. He won't work. Minute he sees a plow he starts swinging back. You can't make him go. Gets that pride from his mama. Everywhere that mare went, he went, followed her everywhere . . . so when he got big . . . he just like her."

When he became an artist, Bill liked to sketch on old, throwaway cardboard. The creases, torn edges, and dirty smudges helped him decide what to draw. Before Bill drew *Man with Mule Plowing*, he looked carefully at the shape of the cardboard. The curve in the upper left-hand corner made him think of a hat. The sloping angle on the right reminded him of a mule's head.

Most Black Belt families were poor and had to work as hard as their mules to survive.

But after a day in the fields, the people rested themselves. The men went fishing or possum hunting, and the women sewed clothes or pieced quilts. On hot summer days, children splashed and played in the Alabama River. There was no money to buy toys, so they made up their own games.

Bill's youngsters would have scrunched down on the edge of the creek to watch crawfish swim by. But they made sure they kept their hands out of reach. Alabama children believed that when a crawfish bit, it clamped down until it heard thunder.

Like other young folks in the Black Belt, the Traylor children probably liked to build frog houses. First, they piled wet sand over their closed fists. Then they carefully removed their hands to leave a hollow space. Bruh Frog, however, never seemed to want to move into his new home.

If Bill's cabin had a dogtrot, the family gathered there to catch a breeze, sing ballads, and tell stories. Like mosquitoes in a pond, folktales multiplied on warm summer nights.

Yarns about the folk hero Railroad Bill were a favorite in the Black Belt. He was the African-American Robin Hood of Alabama in the 1890s. According to legend, Railroad Bill had killed a sheriff and become a "woods-rider," or outlaw. It was said that he robbed banks, then left food in the middle of the night for hungry Black Belt farmers.

People loved to talk of how Railroad Bill outsmarted the law. When a sheriff tried to catch him, the renegade turned himself into a rabbit or a dog. Scarecrows once helped him rob a night train by holding torches so that he could see.

Like Railroad Bill, the husky blue dog in the painting shown on the next page is poised to defend himself. The startled eye has spotted danger, and the bared fangs are ready to rip the pants off a deputy's leg. Could this fierce dog be Railroad Bill? Perhaps he has tricked the sheriff again!

African Americans who lived around Benton also told scary stories about cats. One former slave believed that a cat could suffocate a baby by sucking its breath. Another said that the owner of a black-cat bone was able to make herself or himself disappear. To cure a cold, some claimed, stew a black cat and drink the gravy.

Bill must have remembered these stories when he drew *Scary Creature*. With its staring eyes, four-fingered arms, and eleven

Bill Traylor once said, "I wanted to be plowing so bad today, I drawed me a man plowing." *Man with Mule Plowing, ca. 1939–1942. Poster paint and pencil on cardboard. 15" x 25½". Collection of Didi and David Barrett. Photograph courtesy Ricco/Maresca Gallery.*

When Bill was growing up, he would have heard that it was bad luck to kill a dog. Perhaps that's why he drew most of his dogs as powerful creatures. *Blue Dog, ca. 1939–1942. Poster paint on cardboard. 12" x 13½". Collection of Judy Saslow.*

spiky teeth, this catlike being does seem to have spooky powers.

Storytelling helped the Traylor family get through workdays. But they all looked forward to the weekend. In 1890 nine hundred forty-two people lived in and around Benton. On Saturday afternoons African-American families hooked their mules to their wagons and rode to town.

The women visited and bought supplies of sugar, coffee, molasses, and chewing tobacco. The men threw dice in the back of the store. Young people courted while children played in the sandy lanes. And they all ate fried fish or steak bought in the street market.

Making "shinny," or illegal moonshine liquor, was a common pastime in Alabama. Saturday-night frolics started out in a neighbor's house or a cleared field in the countryside. Refreshments were sold, a fiddler and guitarist played for money or food, and square dancing followed. But too many sips of corn liquor could turn a party into a fight.

Bill remembered this part of his past in

Scary Creature, ca. 1939–1942. Compressed charcoal on cardboard. 17¾" x 10⅜". Collection of the Montgomery Museum of Fine Arts, Montgomery, Alabama. Gift of Charles and Eugenia Shannon.

Bill knew and understood animals so well that he often made them bigger and more lifelike than people. *Exciting Event, Hunters and Drinkers, ca. 1939–1942. Colored pencil and pencil on cardboard, 15″ x 20″. Collection of Joan Lowenthal. Photograph courtesy Ricco/Maresca Gallery.*

Exciting Event, Hunters and Drinkers. The scene has all the ingredients of a Saturday-night brawl: drinking, chasing, and fussing. The man in the hat is getting a lecture from his wife. As Bill once said of a nagging woman he had drawn, "She's not asking him where he's been, she's telling him." Two impish figures poke the pair to get their attention. Perhaps they are the couple's children.

The hunter may be Bill Traylor. He is in the center of the action but is not a part of it. He seems to watch the spectacle with regret. "What little sense I did have," Bill once said, "whiskey took away."

TURN OF THE CENTURY

"I woke up this morning, these blues all
   round my bed.
Couldn't eat my breakfast, and there's blues
   all in my bread."

Lonesome Home Blues

Bill turned forty-four in 1900. By this time he had witnessed the bloodbath of civil war and the end of two hundred fifty years of slavery in the United States. Yet some things had stayed the same for him, and others had gotten worse.

He had been forbidden to learn to read and write as a slave. Now he still had no way to learn his letters. Most of the log-cabin schools built by the Freedmen's Bureau in the 1860s had been burned by the Ku Klux Klan. The few that remained were taught by underpaid teachers with one textbook for every five children. Seventy-five percent of black Alabamians couldn't read or write in 1880, along with 25 percent of whites.

Lynchings had replaced the whippings of slavery. Between 1889 and 1918, 237 African Americans in Bill's state were illegally executed for imagined crimes, including poisoning a mule. And in 1901, lawmakers made it impossible for Bill to vote. Only male property owners who could read and write were allowed to go to the polls. There were over six thousand registered voters in Bill's county in 1905. Fifty-seven of them were black, but he was not one of them.

Bill and other former slaves watched their promise of freedom fade away. To escape poverty, violence, and illiteracy, many continued to migrate to the North. Most,

Alabama moonshiners made illegal whiskey in barrels such as this one. *Drinkers with Keg. ca. 1939–1942. Pencil on cardboard. 10½" x 14⅝". Collection of Judy Saslow.*

though, found poor housing, unemployment, and prejudice when they got there. For those who stayed behind, music was one of the best ways to forget hardship.

African Americans had always used music to lighten their load. During slavery times in Alabama, a religious "shout" song had accompanied movements called the Heavenly Dance. The rhythmic singing and walking had carried troubled slaves to a better place, if only in their thoughts.

Work songs made a job easier. The beat of a song helped Bill lift heavy bales of cotton onto a wagon. And if Lorisa spun thread or wove baskets, she repeated the same hand motions hundreds of times. The rhythm of a song chased her boredom away.

When Bill worked outside, he might have called for a tool or a drink of water with a field holler. Hollers gave workers who were spread out over many acres a way to talk to one another. Their slow, drawling cries curled through the fields, rising and falling like waves in the still summer air.

Singing also provided amusement for African Americans. Before the Civil War, Bruh Rabbit and his animal friends appeared in "ballits," or songs that told a story. After the war, superstrong men like John Henry were the heroes of African-American ballads.

Shouts, work songs, hollers, ballads—by 1900 American blacks had created a rich musical stew of songs with an African taste. Then Black Belt guitar players combined these song rhythms with the bleak realities of their lives. By 1910 a new kind of music had been born: the country blues.

For the next forty years, Bill Traylor listened to the blues. He may have first heard them played by migrant laborers from Mississippi and Louisiana who rambled throughout the Deep South looking for work. They carried their guitars, or "boxes," and spread the blues like seeds on the wind.

Later Bill heard lonely blues chords on records. Few black farming families had radios. By the 1920s, however, between 10 and 20 percent had their own phonographs. Like the cassette players of today, it was easy to carry a phonograph to a party or picnic.

He might also have heard the blues played in roadside bars called barrelhouses, or in juke joints built on the edge of town. As sad as a rainy day, the blues worked their way into Bill Traylor's mind and back out through his art.

At first the verses in a blues song seem unrelated, like the scattered figures in one of Bill's pictures. They don't tell a story with beginning, middle, and end. But the words, like Bill's images, do paint a picture of Black Belt life: men and women who love and leave, feeling broke and feeling bad, judges and jails, mules and moonshine whiskey.

Singers used the same topics over and over in their songs. "Everything that happened to one person has at some time or other happened to another one," said a blues artist about blues lyrics. "If not, it will."

Bill, too, repeated animals, houses, and people in his art. Yet every blues song, like every Traylor drawing, is a new episode. Each is a fresh way of telling what it was like to be an African American in the Black Belt community.

Blues songs are often about travel by bus or train:

Here come number three with her headlight
    turned down.
I believe to my soul she's Alabama bound.

The same theme of restless wandering appears in *House with Figures and Animals*.

Everything in the picture is on the move.

Bill said that the lines at the top of the drawing were meant to be a fence. *Untitled (House with Figures and Animals), ca. 1939–1942. Colored pencil on cardboard. 22" x 13½". Courtesy Luise Ross Gallery, New York.*

A horse balks at the fence that runs behind the cabin. As it gallops across the cardboard, the horse tries to pull the figure on the roof along with it. The bird is ready to take flight, and the one-legged man won't stay put, either. With his cane and crutch, he edges toward the bottom of the drawing. A snake wiggles through the middle of the confusion.

The Boxers is also like a blues song. A typical country blues musician made up verses while he sang. Pauses in the music gave him time to think of new words. Bill, too, put exactly the right amount of space between the images in his art. The figures in the picture are separated by a kind of visual pause. Each character stands alone. But the gap is narrow, and we know from the fighters' stares that a strong emotion connects them.

Some say that the blues grew out of African Americans' strong religious faith. Church-going was a key part of African-American culture, like singing and storytelling. From Bill's two pictures of a black Jesus and his four drawings of preachers, we know that religion left its mark on him.

In *Preacher and Congregation* the artist shows the importance of community in

Bill may have been thinking of the African-American boxer Joe Louis when he painted this picture. Louis won the world heavyweight championship in 1937. Called "The Brown Bomber," he was born in Alabama and was the son of a sharecropper. *Boxers in Blue, ca. 1939–1942. Poster paint and pencil on cardboard. 20⅞" x 22". Collection of Judy Saslow.*

African-American culture. Religion, like the blues, gave the people a psychic home—a time and place to share their feelings. This minister is not separated from his flock by a distant pulpit. Instead, he is in the center because the people have accepted him as their guide. They worship together as a group: The preacher calls out a prayer, and they agree, "Amen!"

Like two train rails, Bill's life and the blues ran side by side. Each was born in the nineteenth century and matured in the twentieth. There is a sweet sorrow in both, but the pain is balanced by a spicy humor. And just as the blues moved from cabin porches to juke joints, Bill Traylor had to leave the familiar cow paths around Benton for the hard streets of the city.

On Sundays black congregations in Bill's county sang, "Oh, where you runnin', sinner, you can't hide!" *Preacher and Congregation, ca. 1939–1942. Pencil and colored pencil on paper. 15¼" x 13¼". Collection of Judy Saslow.*

MONTGOMERY

"My mother's dead, my father's crossed the
    sea,
Ain't got nobody to feel and care for me."

Blues verse

By 1900 the number of people living in Benton had risen to 1,094. Cotton production continued to rise. In 1902 farmers in Bill's county grew over fifteen million pounds of cotton. But too many years of growing cotton robbed the soil of nutrients and made it unfit for raising anything else. Within thirty years, Black Belt dirt was as worn out as the farmers who plowed it.

Only 757 people were left in Benton when the Depression started in 1930. By the end of that decade, over half of those people were gone, too, including Bill's family. His life turned a lonely corner.

Lorisa had died sometime after 1900. Their children had grown up and moved on. One daughter, Esther, went to Detroit, Michigan, to run a boardinghouse. Another daughter, Sarah, lived in nearby Montgomery. Others left for Pittsburgh, Cleveland, and Washington, D.C.

An elderly Black Belt farmer like Bill often became a "casual." Casuals labored in the fields for a "hand's share," or a load of corn and potatoes. But they earned no money.

When Marion Traylor's widow died in 1934, even this meager life would have ended for seventy-eight-year-old Bill. "My white folks had died," Bill remembered later, "and my children scattered." He began to think about leaving the cabin by the creek.

Sometime in the mid-1930s, Bill Traylor traveled east on U.S. Highway 80, probably in a wagon. Bill crossed Big Swampy Creek, rolled past crumbling mansions, and saw hogs shoveling their snouts into clover fields along the road. Thirty-five miles later, the wagon clattered over the Pintialla River bridge. Bill was only a few miles from his new home of Montgomery, Alabama.

He worked briefly in a shoe factory in Montgomery. When rheumatism forced him to quit, he received fifteen dollars a month from welfare. At first he may have lived in his daughter's house. But perhaps Bill couldn't resist the excitement of the city's African-American business district. The streets were alive with shops, fish markets, restaurants ("Rice and big mullet or mackerel fish,

$.30"), and a clothing store located "just around the corner from high prices."

Or maybe Bill simply longed to live on his own again. In 1939 he spent his days sitting on a box on Monroe Street, five blocks from the Alabama River. At night he moved into the back room of the Ross Clayton Funeral Parlor, where empty coffins stood on end like a crowd of mummies. Bill shoved the boxes aside to clear a ten-foot space for his six-foot, four-inch frame. Then he unrolled some rags to make a bed for himself on the floor and dreamed of all he had seen that day.

If life is a play, Bill Traylor's box on Monroe Street was the best seat in the house. A board fence stood between him and a blacksmith's shop, but he could still hear the clink of horseshoes and the clang of hammers on anvils. These were background music for scenes that unfolded on the sidewalk set in front of him each day.

Across the street was a small hotel. Mexican and African-American migrant workers arrived at the nearby train and bus stations. Suitcases in hand, they passed Bill on their way to rent rooms, like actors crossing a stage.

On Saturdays farmers rode to town in mule-drawn wagons. After shopping and visiting, the men slipped into the pool hall for beer. But first they asked their friend, Bill, to guard the bags of feed and jugs of kerosene that they left at his feet.

He made friends with several one-legged men. He also knew a legless fellow named Jimmie, who pushed himself around on a rocker stool. Children were drawn to Bill, as were drifters who passed through the area looking for work. One drifter taught Bill the alphabet and how to write his name. With a halo of white hair circling his bald head and a generous face, Bill Traylor was a magnet for the people of the street.

We don't know when or why he started to draw. Maybe the rough clamor of street life excited his imagination. Or perhaps he felt lonely and needed to bring some of his many memories to life. One day Bill Traylor picked up an old cardboard advertisement and the stub of a pencil. A stream of drawings began at that moment. Forty years later they entered the current of American art.

After Bill learned the alphabet, he enjoyed painting letters. *Blue Man Reading, ca. 1939–1942. Poster paint on cardboard. 11½" x 7¾". Collection of Judy Saslow.*

The details of this drawing show that Bill was quite familiar with blacksmithing tools and techniques. *Blacksmith Shop, ca. 1939–1942. Pencil on cardboard. 13⅜" x 26¼". Collection of Charles Shannon.*

TWO ARTISTS

"I got the world in a jug, the stopper in my hand."

Blues verse

One early summer day in 1939, a twenty-four-year-old man named Charles Shannon left the log-cabin studio he had built in the country. He climbed into his car and drove forty miles to Montgomery for a weekend visit.

Charles first strolled through the downtown area and past the courthouse-square fountain. Then he walked to the African-American part of town—a lively community that he called "a world unto itself." And since he was an artist, he made notes, sketches, and photographs of all that he observed.

When he reached Monroe Street, he noticed an old man on a box. The fellow was drawing with a three-inch pencil stub. "He was sitting on a sidewalk, making marks on paper," remembered Charles. "He was an interesting-looking man. His hands were big, strong, capable hands."

The young artist sat quietly and watched eighty-five-year-old Bill Traylor draw. He was intrigued by the simplicity of Bill's methods and materials. The older artist balanced a drawing board in his lap. He held a three-inch block of wood in his left hand. With his right, he drew straight lines against the edge of the wood.

Later Bill added pictures of rats, cats, shoes, cups, and teakettles. As small as Cracker Jack toys, the tiny objects marched across the page in even formation.

To draw the torso of a person or large animal, Bill first drew the straight lines of a rectangle, as shown in *Mean Dog*. Then he turned the rectangle into a body by rounding out the edges with his pencil, freehand. Long triangles became a neck, arms, and legs in the same way.

Bill didn't know how to make pictures that showed the depth of an object. So he invented his own flat style of drawing. To show both eyes on a person or animal, he simply twisted the whole head around on the body. When he drew white people, he outlined a face, but didn't shade it in.

Shortly after Charles discovered his "people's artist," Bill moved over to North Law-

The faint ruled lines show that Bill began by drawing a simple rectangle. *Mean Dog, ca. 1939–1942. Poster paint and pencil on paper. 22" x 28". Collection of Judy Saslow.*

rence Street. Each night he slept on the floor of a shoe-repair shop. In the morning he moved outside, ten steps away. The overhang off the back entrance to a pool hall sheltered him from the rain, and he stored his artwork behind a Coca-Cola ice chest. This spot was home to him for the next three years. Here, until 1942, he produced his best work.

Two weeks after Bill moved, Charles brought him brushes, thick poster board, colored pencils, and bright poster paint. Other friends gave him crayons and charcoal sticks. Bill ignored the poster board. He preferred to draw on the back of a cigarette advertisement or a Baby Ruth candy-bar box.

He used many of the pencils and crayons, but only a few of the poster paints. The artist didn't mix paint. Sometimes he added water, but he liked strong colors and usually dipped the brush straight into the jar. His favorite shades were bright reds, dark browns, and deep blues.

Using the light that hung by the doorway,

Bill told how he drew a white face. He laid his stick down on the profile and said, "When the stick touches the nose and chin but it doesn't touch the lips, it's a white man." *Mexican Woman with Handbag, ca. 1939–1942. Pencil on cardboard. 14" x 6½". Collection of Judy Saslow.*

Bill sometimes drew until ten o'clock at night. As he sketched he calmly smoked a patched pipe. "He never agonized over his work," Charles remembered. "He was very serene. . . . He just started out and worked to a conclusion. He didn't fuss with things."

Bill had fun with his art and laughed at his own pictures. "Look at that man 'bout to hit that chicken," he said of one busy scene. "That's a ruckus," he said of another. Once the artist drew a picture of Ross Clayton, the undertaker, and joked, "When he comes in, he always looks around seein' if them boxes is empty."

One day Bill decided that other people might enjoy his drawings. He tied string to them and hung them on a nearby fence. When they began to sell (for less than ten cents each), this amused Bill, too. "Sometimes they buys 'em when they don't even need 'em," he said.

Like many untrained artists, Bill didn't sketch because he wanted money. He drew from a different kind of need. By remem-

The stooped posture reveals that Bill felt the weight of his many years. The shoes, pipe, and hat give dignity to the figure. *Self-Portrait with Pipe, ca. 1939–1942. Pencil and colored pencil on cardboard. 7⅞" x 11½". Collection of Siri von Reis. Photograph courtesy Ricco/Maresca Gallery.*

bering his younger years through art, he made his old age easier.

The following winter Charles brought some exciting news to Bill. He had arranged for the New South Art Center to hold a one-man show of Bill's drawings. But Bill had not become an artist in order to become famous. He wasn't very impressed by the announcement. "Uh-huh" was his only reply.

On Sunday, February 11, 1940, members of the New South met at 4:00 P.M. in an old cotton-market building in downtown Montgomery. There was a catalog to assemble for Bill's exhibit, with covers of cardboard and pages made from brown wrapping paper. The group must have also decided how to transport Bill from his streetside home to the center. They would have spent the rest of the day hanging his pictures for the show.

On Monday Charles drove Bill to the center. The elderly artist slowly started up the two flights of steep steps. Even with two canes and Charles's help, it was a painful half-hour climb.

When they finally reached the third floor, Bill looked around. Sunlight floated down through skylights and brushed the blue walls with a pale, wintry glow. One hundred draw-ings lined the two rooms of the center, in-cluding an exuberant yellow chicken that seemed to dance off the paper and into the air.

Bill walked around the rooms one time, gazed at each picture as if he had never seen it before, and announced that he was ready to leave. He cared nothing for an exhibit of his art. It was the making of art that brought him satisfaction. "Nobody was less im-pressed with Bill Traylor," recalled Charles, "than he was with himself."

Charles had been so moved by Bill that he had painted a huge eight-foot by four-foot mural of him. This hung on the wall of the exhibit, too. Most people would be fasci-nated by their own portraits. But from what we know of Bill, he probably glanced at the image of himself, made a quiet joke about the man in the picture, and limped away.

Charles Shannon was dedicated to show-ing Bill's art to the rest of the world. He visited New York museums and brought some of Bill's pictures with him. When Charles told Bill that the staff at the Museum of Modern Art liked his art, Bill simply an-swered, "They did?"

Then Charles arranged another one-man

show at a school in New York. Bill received a ten-dollar fee for the loan of his pictures. This was only the second, and the last, public display of the artist's work while he was still alive.

Some art critics see the soul of Africa in Bill's art. They mention a resemblance between his pictures and prehistoric rock engravings found in the Sahara Desert. Like Bill, these primitive artists drew agile animals that seem ready to leap off the surface of the rock.

Bill's style also reminds people of ancient African art from Egypt. The Egyptians painted the front view of a face on a body that was turned sideways. In a similar way *Black Cat* tiptoes over to the right of the page, while its head gazes directly at the viewer.

As did Egyptian artists, Bill gave a figure importance just by making it larger. In *Man and Large Dog* a small man leads a giant dog. Perhaps Bill made the dog bigger because animals were such a vital part of his world.

He also felt a special connection to birds.

Bill may have played a game called Chick-a-ma, Chick-a-ma, Craina Crow when he was a child. In this game, the "witch" (leader) steals "chickens" (children) and pretends to eat them. *Yellow Chicken, ca. 1939–1942. Poster paint and pencil on cardboard. 13⅞" x 8¼". Collection of Eugenia Shannon.*

Charles Shannon called Bill's work "the most joyous art I've ever seen." *Black Cat, ca. 1939–1942. Poster paint on cardboard. 8" x 10". Collection of Judy Saslow.*

In West Africa, birds are a symbol of the mind. They are frequently seen on the tops of statues and carvings. In a book of one hundred fifty of Bill's pictures, birds appear in almost half of the drawings. Chickens strut and crows perch throughout his art, and the action in the picture is often centered around them.

West Africans use their carving and basketry skills to make art out of useful items such as bowls, pipes, stools, and baskets. Bill, too, made art from ordinary things when he drew shoes, hats, umbrellas, and drinking flasks. Instead of creating art from actual objects, he turned pictures of objects into art.

Bill may have watched his parents or grandparents carve, weave, or draw. He might also have seen art made by people brought directly from Africa. Slaves born in America usually avoided enslaved Africans. The new arrivals spoke strange-sounding languages and seemed very different. Still, it's quite possible that Bill met Africans sometime in his life. This would have been especially true after emancipation, when newly freed slaves became so mobile.

For example, an African woman with the American name of Gracie McQueen lived

Bill often used both sides of blank cardboard. He painted a man and woman on the back of this picture. *Untitled (Man and Large Dog), ca. 1939–1942. Pencil and showcard color on cardboard. 28" x 22". Courtesy Luise Ross Gallery, New York.*

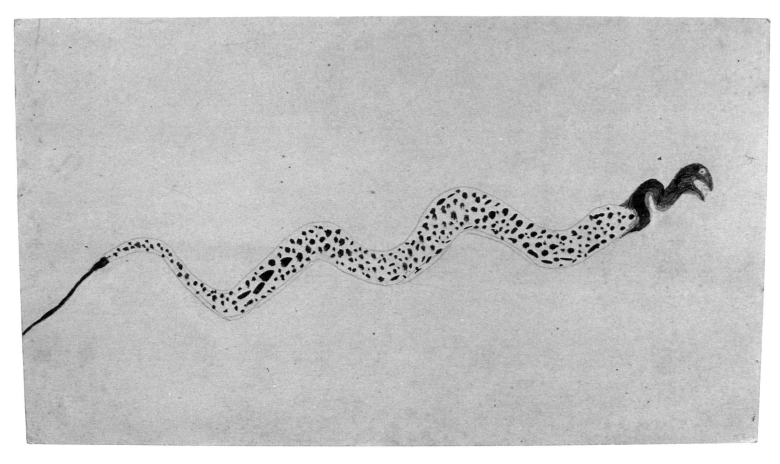

African Americans in Bill's county told many tales about snakes, and he often included snakes in his art. He would have heard that if you rub a snake "shed," or skin, in your hand, you won't break any dishes. *Spotted Snake, ca. 1939–1942. Pencil and gouache on paper. 26" x 31", framed. Collection of Judy Saslow.*

only fifteen miles from Benton. She died at the age of 110, when Bill was 19 years old.

And in the 1930s, an 85-year-old former slave remembered the "saltwater" people who worked in fields near Selma, twelve miles from Benton. "I was with the Africans," she said. "They couldn't understand what they was saying theyselves. . . . When you made one of 'em mad you made all of 'em mad."

Art historians are fascinated by the similarities between African-American and African art. But was there an African influence on Bill's art? Why he drew as he did will always be a riddle. We only know that Bill, as Charles Shannon once said, "reached deep within to find his expression."

WORLD WAR II AND AFTER

"I'm settin' here wonderin' will a matchbox
    hold my clothes.
  I ain't got so many matches but I got so
    far to go."

Matchbox Blues

American armed forces entered World War II in December 1941. The war turned life upside down for everyone, including Charles Shannon and Bill Traylor. Charles's visits to Bill stopped after he was drafted into the army in June 1942. The younger man spent the war years in the South Pacific. Bill led the wandering life of a gypsy. Too restless to stay in one place, he lived with children in Chicago, Detroit, New York, Philadelphia, and Washington, D.C. It would be four long years before the two friends saw each other again.

The war finally ended in 1945. But when Charles returned to Alabama, nothing looked the same. "All the little houses in the country were empty," he remembered, "and starting to blow away." Many of the farmers had left to work in northern factories. Cattle now grazed where cotton used to grow.

One day in January 1946, Charles returned to the same boarded-up back door behind the pool hall on North Lawrence Street. There he found Bill sitting in his old place as if the war had never happened. But the years had been hard on the older man.

"He looked bad," Charles recalled. The rheumatism in Bill's leg had led to gangrene, and doctors had amputated the limb. "I begged them not to cut it off," Bill told

Charles. "I told them I wanted to go out like I come in."

Shortly after Charles found Bill in his old spot, the welfare agency made the elderly artist move in with his daughter Sarah. "He felt awfully abused," Charles said. "He'd sit in his daughter's backyard under a fig tree and try to draw. But he wasn't happy. He wanted to be on the street."

Bill's pictures from these years show the strain of a frustrated artist. He just couldn't draw, he said, "with all the fuss going on." And, perhaps because he had lost mobility himself, the figures that he drew had no grace and movement. They looked as Bill must have felt—stiff and awkward.

About a year later Charles received a letter dictated by Bill. "Dear Sir," it read. "I am asking you to come to the Fraternal Hospital, 42 Dorsey Street, Montgomery. I want to see you at once. Yours truly, Bill Traylor." Charles found Bill lying on a cot in a large ward filled with a dozen other patients. The two artists were able to share one last visit, although Bill was too sick to talk.

Sometime later, Bill's daughter called Charles. Her father had passed on, she said, and was already buried. It is not certain when Bill Traylor died. Some say he passed away in February 1947, but there is a photograph of him that is dated 1948. A great-granddaughter recalls that she was born around the time of Bill's death, in October 1949.

No matter the year, America lost a remarkable artist and a gentle man on the day Bill Traylor left this earth. "A kind of beautiful simplicity came through," Charles said of his friend, "a selflessness." Bill Traylor was a man who "was right with himself."

AFTERWORD

"My strongest trial now is past, my triumph just begun."

Slave spiritual

One day in the mid-1970s, Charles Shannon dragged some old boxes out of storage. Over a thousand of Bill's pictures were waiting inside, like ivy growing under last year's leaves. For a quarter of a century, the artist had saved Bill Traylor's drawings. Now he wanted his wife, Eugenia, to see them.

Charles sifted through the pieces of old cardboard. Memories of an old man on a box and an early summer day in 1939 wandered through his mind. The pictures were still marvelous, Charles decided, and his wife agreed. "Thus began a second life for Gina and me," remembers Charles. Together they spent the next five years cleaning the drawings and making lists of them.

The Shannons made slides of Bill's art and took them to museums and art dealers. In 1979 they finally saw Bill's work accepted by the art world when a one-man show opened in a New York art gallery. Then a museum chose Bill's drawing of a coiled snake for the cover of its exhibit catalog *Black Folk Art in America*. When art lovers saw the thirty-six Traylor pictures included in the exhibit, they pronounced him the star of the show.

His works have been seen in over twenty-five one-man exhibitions and over sixty-six group exhibitions, from New York to Los Angeles, Chicago to New Orleans, Japan to Sweden. People all over the world have now shared the joy and wit of Bill Traylor, an African-American artist who taught himself how to draw.

A circus poster may have inspired this painting. *Black Elephant with Brown Ear, ca. 1939–1942. Poster paint on cardboard. 14¾" x 26". Collection of Lanford Wilson.*